CUBE
BOOK

WONDERS OF THE
HOLY LAND

WHITE STAR PUBLISHERS

text by
CARLO GIORGI

graphic layout
PAOLA PIACCO

editorial coordination
LAURA ACCOMAZZO
VALENTINA GIAMMARINARO
FEDERICA ROMAGNOLI

translation
SALVATORE CIOLFI

editing
SUZANNE SMITHER

© 2011 EDIZIONI WHITE STAR S.R.L.
VIA M. GERMANO, 10
13100 VERCELLI - ITALY
WWW.WHITESTAR.IT

The port of Akko, which is dominated by the Ottoman citadel.

ISBN 978-88-544-0609-4

1 2 3 4 5 6   15 14 13 12 11

Printed in China

CONTENTS

WONDERS OF THE HOLY LAND

1 • The city of Jerusalem is represented in a Byzantine mosaic in the Church of St. George in Madaba, Jordan.

2-3 • The setting sun illuminates the fortress of Masada, conquered by the Roman armies only after a siege that lasted nearly three years.

4-5 • The walls of Suleiman the Magnificent, built in 1542 to defend Jerusalem, glisten in the sunset.

6-7 • Farms, fields and human settlements draw regular geometry in the fertile Jordan Valley.

11 • The Mosque of Omar and the Armenian Catholic Church of Saint Mary, stretched out under the same sky, are a sign of Jerusalem's religious wealth.

12-13 • The imposing and columned Roman Amphitheatre in Beit She'an is among the most impressive archaeological sights of Israel.

14-15 • Religious faithful crowded at the Western Wall or Wailing Wall. On the left are the men, on the right the women.

Introduction

CAN LAND BE HOLY? CAN WE SPEAK OF THINGS ON A SACRED, HIGHER PLANE WITHOUT IGNORING THE ROUGHNESS AND PHYSICALITY OF EVERYDAY LIFE? THERE IS AT LEAST ONE PLACE ON THE PLANET FOR WHICH THE ANSWER IS YES. THAT PLACE IS THE HOLY LAND. HERE THE TRAVELER CAN ONLY SURRENDER TO A REALITY IN WHICH GREAT, SEEMINGLY IRRECONCILABLE CONTRASTS (LIKE THE HEAVENS AND THE EARTH) COEXIST NATURALLY. THIS IS THE PLACE WHERE YOU CAN FIND, IN EQUAL MEASURE, A MODERN FOCUS BASED ON FUTURISTIC ARCHITECTURE AND CUTTING EDGE TECHNOLOGY AND A TRADITION ROOTED IN MILLENNIA OF HISTORY. THIS IS LAND IDENTIFIABLE BY

17 ● Perched on the mountainside like a fortress, the monastery of Mar Saba shines behind its blue domes.

Introduction

BOTH THE MODERN SKYSCRAPERS OF TEL AVIV AND THE COLORFUL SOUKS OF DAMASCUS, A REGION TO ADMIRE FOR THE ARCHAEOLOGICAL WONDERS OF PETRA, PALMYRA AND JERICHO, THE BOULEVARDS OF BEIRUT OR THE TECHNOLOGICALLY ADVANCED KIBBUTZ IN NEGEV THAT ALLOW THE ARID DESERT TO MIRACULOUSLY BLOOM. THIS IS LAND THAT IS HOME, IN EQUAL MEASURE, TO THE SPIRIT AND THE FLESH. HOME TO THE THREE GREAT MONOTHEISTIC RELIGIONS, JUDAISM, CHRISTIANITY AND ISLAM, WHERE ABRAHAM, JESUS AND THE EARLY FOLLOWERS OF MUHAMMAD ALL LIVED AND WALKED. IT IS A PLACE OF REVERED SHRINES AND PRAYER, OF MINARETS AND STEEPLES THAT ACT AS AN INVOCATION TO HEAVEN;

Introduction

DESERTS CHOSEN FOR THE SOUL'S ASCENT, AND ONE OF THE MOST VISITED DESTINATIONS FOR PILGRIMS. IT IS, HOWEVER, ALSO THE LAND OF EPOCHAL WARS, WHICH HAVE SEEN CROSSED SWORDS AND THE SPILT BLOOD OF CRUSADERS AND OTTOMANS, SIEGES AND MASSACRES, CONQUESTS AND DESTRUCTION, UP TO AND INCLUDING THE MOST RECENT PAINFUL CONFLICTS THAT STILL HAVE NO SOLUTION.

IF THIS LAND, DESPITE EVERYTHING, IS VISITED BY THE SPIRIT AND IS HOLY, THEN, MORE THAN ANY OTHER, IT IS IRREPLACEABLE. AFTER ALL, THE HOLY LAND IS THE "FRONT DOOR" OF HUMANITY, THE DOOR THAT THE WEST HAS TO GO THROUGH TO UNDERSTAND THE MYSTERIES AND COMPLEXITIES OF THE EAST, AND VICE

Introduction

VERSA. FOR THOUSANDS OF YEARS, EAST AND WEST HAVE MET BETWEEN THE NILE AND THE EUPHRATES AS WARRIORS, MERCHANTS OR PILGRIMS. IN ROMAN TIMES, THE SPICE ROUTE LEADING TO CHINA BEGAN HERE, AND THIS TRADITION CONTINUED INTO THE LAST CENTURY, WITH THE SUEZ CANAL OPENING A BRAND NEW, REVOLUTIONARY COMMERCIAL CORRIDOR. BUT THIS CLASH OF FAITHS AND PEOPLE CAN BE, ABOVE ALL ELSE, THE GATEWAY TO DIALOGUE AMONG CIVILIZATIONS. IT CAN BECOME A MEETING PLACE RATHER THAN A BATTLEGROUND. IT CAN REMOVE THE OXYGEN FROM THE FUNDAMENTALISM PRESENT IN DIFFERENT FAITHS AND

22-23 ● On the Mount of Olives you will notice, from left to right, the Basilica of the Agony, the golden domes of the Monastery of Russian Orthodox Nuns and the Sanctuary of Dominus Flevit.

Introduction

AFFIRMS THE PRIMACY OF EVERYDAY LIVING AND RELIGIOUS FREEDOM.

THIS IS THE LAND, FINALLY, OF "BIG DREAMS": THE PLACE THE JEWISH POPULATION HAS YEARNED FOR INCESSANTLY IN THE CENTURIES OF ITS DIASPORA, A DESTINATION FOR CHRISTIAN PILGRIMS SINCE THE MIDDLE AGES, AND A HOLY PLACE FOR MUSLIMS. IT HAS BEEN THE BELOVED SETTING OF EPIC STORIES AND TALES, IN WHICH GENIES, SULTANS AND MAGIC LAMPS CONTINUE TO SPARK THE IMAGINATION OF GENERATIONS OF ADULTS AND CHILDREN. IT IS THE LAND OF SHARED DREAMS, WITH ONE STILL TO BE FULFILLED: THAT OF PEACE.

24-25 • The sunny valley in which the Dead Sea lies is over 1,300 feet below sea level. On the horizon one can see the hills of Jordan.

JERUSALEM
of GOLD

- The so-called "Tower of David" stands out from the old city walls. Despite the name, it is a minaret built during the Ottoman-Turk occupation in the 17th century.

INTRODUCTION Jerusalem of Gold

IF THERE IS A CITY IN THE WORLD THAT BEST SYM-
BOLIZES THE HISTORY OF MEN SEARCHING FOR GOD, ONE
THAT REPRESENTS THE SOMETIMES PAINFUL, BUT ESSENTIAL,
COEXISTENCE BETWEEN DIFFERENT CULTURES, BELIEFS AND
PEOPLE, IT IS JERUSALEM. "IF I FORGET THEE, O JERUSALEM,
MAY MY RIGHT HAND FORGET ME," (PSALM 137) SANG THE
PSALMIST MANY CENTURIES AGO, FROM EXILE IN BABYLON.
EVEN TODAY, THIS SENTIMENT EXISTS IN THE CHILDREN OF
THE THREE GREAT MONOTHEISTIC RELIGIONS: JEWS, MUS-
LIMS AND CHRISTIANS. DIFFERENT, BUT UNITED IN "HOLY"
JERUSALEM, A HOME NOBODY IS WILLING TO GIVE UP.
TODAY WE ENTER JERUSALEM THROUGH IMPOSING ROADS
THAT FUNNEL TRAFFIC INTO THE CITY. TO THE WEST LIES THE
NEW CITY OF THE MODERN STATE OF ISRAEL, ORDERED AND

● A massive tower from the 12th century stands next to the Romanesque facade
of the most important church in Christendom, that of the Holy Sepulchre in Jerusalem.

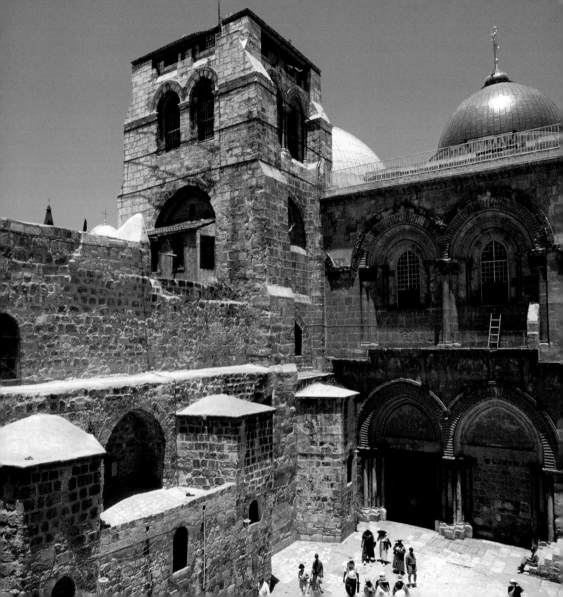

INTRODUCTION Jerusalem of Gold

AS TECHNOLOGICALLY ADVANCED AS A MITTEL-EUROPEAN METROPOLIS; IN THE EAST, THE ARAB CITY, OVERCROWDED AND CLOSED BY SETTLEMENTS, IS MUCH POORER. BETWEEN THESE TWO EXTREMES LIES THE HEART OF JERUSALEM: THE "OLD TOWN," PRESERVED IN ITS MAGIC BY THE POWERFUL ANCIENT WALLS BUILT BY SULEIMAN THE MAGNIFICENT (1542). THE "OLD CITY," NO BIGGER THAN A MEDIEVAL VILLAGE, IS ACTUALLY THE SPIRITUAL CAPITAL OF THE WORLD: FOR THE JEWS IT IS THE CITY OF KING DAVID, THE MOUNT OF THE HOLY SCRIPTURES WHERE THE FIRST AND SECOND TEMPLES WERE ERECTED. IT IS THE CITY SUNG FROM THE BIBLE, AND DREAMED OF BY JEWS DURING THEIR LONG DIASPORA. AND THE "WESTERN WALL," A REMNANT OF ISRAEL'S ANCIENT SPLENDOR SPARED BY THE RAVAGES OF HISTORY, IS NOW AN OPEN AIR SHRINE OF JUDAISM. JERUSALEM, FOR MUSLIMS, IS

INTRODUCTION Jerusalem of Gold

THE HOLY AL-QUDS. IN ITS MOSQUES THEY HAVE PRAYED TO ALLAH CONTINUOUSLY FOR MORE THAN 1,000 YEARS. FROM HERE, MUHAMMAD ASCENDED TO HEAVEN, AND THE SHIMMERING GOLDEN DOME THAT RECALLS HIS PASSING IS THE UNMISTAKABLE SYMBOL OF THE CITY FOR EVERYONE: TOURISTS, DIPLOMATS AND BELIEVERS. FINALLY, FOR CHRISTIANS, THIS IS THE PLACE OF SALVATION: JESUS DIED HERE AND HIS DISCIPLES SAW HIM FOR THE FIRST TIME AFTER HE ROSE FROM THE DEAD. HERE YOU CAN WALK THE PATH HE WALKED WHILE CARRYING THE CROSS, AND PRAY AT HIS EMPTY TOMB. JUST OUTSIDE THE WALLS, THE UPPER ROOM, WHERE THE LAST SUPPER WAS SHARED, STILL STANDS. OUTSIDE, THE GETHSEMANE, THE GARDEN OF OLIVE TREES WHERE JESUS PRAYED BEFORE BEING ARRESTED, STILL ENDURES.

Jerusalem of Gold
Introduction

IN JERUSALEM, THE SIGNS OF THE THREE FAITHS OVERLAP AND MERGE, CREATING A UNIQUE ATMOSPHERE. THE PRAYER OF THE MUEZZIN INTERTWINES WITH THE BELLS OF CHRISTIAN CHURCHES, AND THEY OVERLAP WITH THE FESTIVE SINGING AND DANCING OF THE JEWS AT THE WESTERN WALL. JERUSALEM IS A PALETTE OF COLORS: WHITE STONE, WITH WHICH EVERYTHING IS BUILT, DAZZLES IN THE MORNING SUN AND TURNS PINK AT SUNSET. THE DARK TONES OF THE HEAD COVERS OF JEWISH LEADERS AND THE ROBES OF CHRISTIAN CLERICS MINGLE WITH THE BRIGHT COLORS OF THE VEILS OF MUSLIM WOMEN AND THE RAINBOW OF SPICES FOR SALE IN THE ARAB SOUK. EVERY DAY HERE IS A UNIQUE SYMPHONY OF OPPOSITES. FORCED, FOR OUR GOOD FORTUNE AND DE-SPITE THEMSELVES, TO LIVE TOGETHER.

• A crowd of men gather to hear the reading of the Torah at a Bar Mitzvah, the initiation into adulthood for young Jewish men.

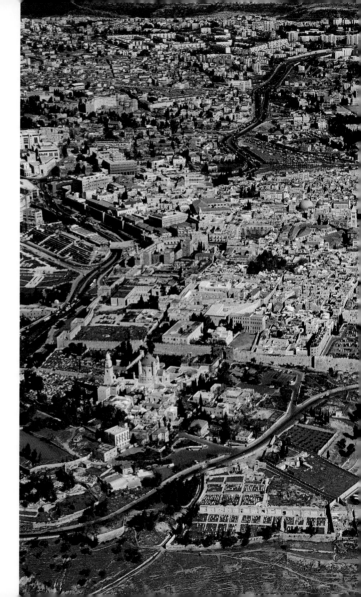

34-35 • Jerusalem "the holy" (al-Quds in Arabic) is built on high ground, over 2,600 feet above sea level. On sunny days, the golden roof of the Mosque of Omar, also known as the Dome of the Rock (from the Arab Qubbat' as-Sakhra), shines like a golden jewel over the city.

36-37 • The Citadel of David has over the centuries been destroyed and rebuilt several times by conquerors and rulers. It was the defensive stronghold of Jerusalem.

38-39 ● The Tower of David, above the Ottoman walls, was erected by Suleiman the Magnificent to make the city impregnable.

39 ● The Jaffa Gate is located near the Tower of David.

After World War II, a number of archaeological excavations were concentrated on the Tower of David, allowing the re-emergence of important vestiges of the city's ancient history.

● The remains of the citadel, illuminated at night, are one of the wonders of Jerusalem seen today by tourists and pilgrims in all their full splendor.

44-45 • The Dung Gate, in the Jewish Quarter, overlooks the Gehenna, the valley where waste from the city was burned in ancient times.

45 • In this view of the massive wall you can appreciate all its grandeur.

Symmetrical, slender and stately spires: the Damascus Gate is the most impressive and monumental entrance to the Old City of Jerusalem.

48 ● Among the most impressive city gates is the Lions' or St. Stephen's Gate.

48-49 ● The Golden Gate, walled up for centuries, is perhaps the most evocative for Muslims, who believe the final judgment will start here.

50 and 50-51 • Between the Mount of Olives and the area of the ancient temple is the Archaeological Park, the most important in Israel, with remains dating back 5,000 years. It includes the Davidson Center, built at the foundation of an Umayyad palace from the 8th century AD.

52-53 • An orderly crowd of Jewish pilgrims waiting to pray by the Western Wall in Jerusalem on a day of celebration.

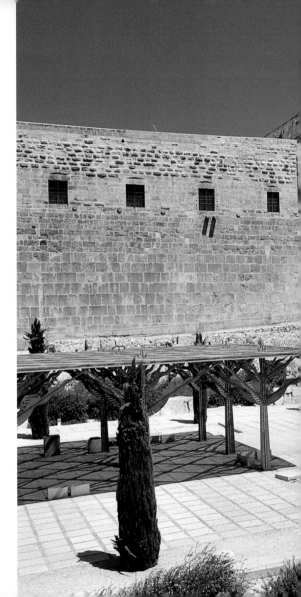

54-55 and 55 • Men and women, separated by a railing, pray facing the Western Wall (also known as the Wailing Wall) which dates back to the Second Temple in Jerusalem, built on the return from Babylon exile in the 6th century BC.

56-57 • Ultra-Orthodox Jews, who wear traditional black clothing, are crowded before the Western Wall during the prayer of the Sabbath.

58-59 ● A Bar Mitzvah, the initiation of young Jews, celebrated in public by friends and relatives in Jerusalem. The Bar Mitzvah is celebrated at the completion of a Jewish boy's 13th year.

59 ● An elderly man carries the Torah scroll.

60 • The public reading of scripture, done for the first time at the Bar Mitzvah, is a symbol of a young Jew's coming of age.

61 • An Orthodox Jew, with head and shoulders covered by the *tallit*, the ritual shawl, raises the Torah scroll.

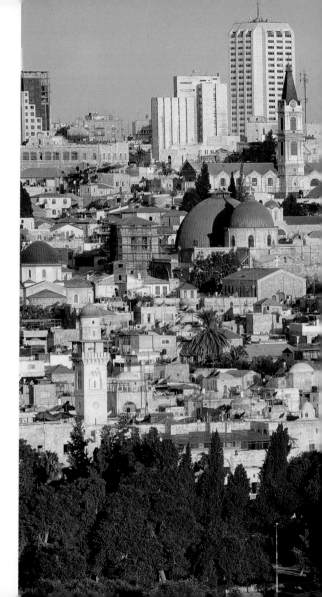

In this view of the city from the Mount of Olives, the skyscrapers of the modern city form a backdrop to the gray domes of the Holy Sepulchre (left) and the golden Dome of the Rock.

64 ● This image of a niche
outside the Mosque of Omar
reveals the splendor of
the decorations.

64-65 ● The mosque, built in the
late 7th century AD, is one of the
oldest places of Islamic worship
in existence.

66-67 ● To enter the mosque, visitors must cross one of these ancient colonnades.

67 ● Due to the brightness of its golden dome, the Mosque of Omar emerges with its distinctive profile in this wide open space.

• Elegant arabesques adorn the walls
and spaces of the old exterior windows
of the Mosque of Omar or Dome
of the Rock.

● Inside the mosque lies the rock that the Islamic tradition venerates as the place from which Muhammad started his miraculous journey to heaven.

The walls of Jerusalem and the golden dome of the Mosque of Omar glow at night, strikingly illuminated by the lights.

The gray dome of the al-Aqsa Mosque, built close to that of Omar in the 8th century, is silhouetted against the backdrop of the old city.

Mighty columns supporting the vaults of the al-Aqsa Mosque, the largest in Jerusalem, which can accommodate up to 5,000 faithful.

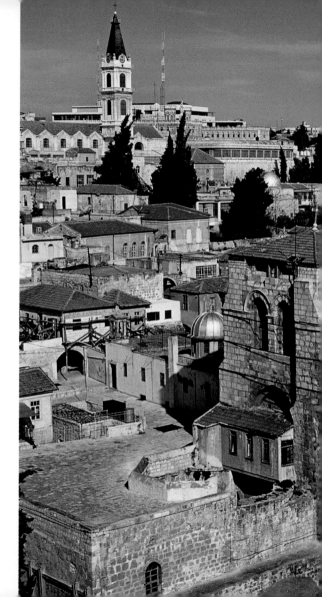

The complex of the Basilica of the Holy Sepulchre stands on the site where Christian tradition places the crucifixion and resurrection of Christ.

80 • A vault adorned by 12 golden rays of light overlooks the shrine of the Holy Sepulchre.

81 • Easter candles, hanging lamps and paintings depicting the resurrection decorate the entrance to the place where it is believed that Christ was buried.

82 • The Stone of Unction recalls the deposition of the crucified body of Christ and its anointing at the hands of Nicodemus and Joseph of Arimathea.

83 • The so-called "chorus of the Greeks" is the central part of the Holy Sepulchre, where the Orthodox rites are celebrated.

In the light of candles
and oil lamps, a rite
is celebrated in the
underground chapel
of St. Helena in the
Basilica of the
Holy Sepulchre.

86 ◈ In the Chapel of Calvary, the altar where Christian pilgrims kneel is located directly on the rock that held the cross of Christ.

87 ◈ The altar is surmounted by an image of the crucifixion, made according to the decorative style of the Eastern Churches.

88-89 • This shop in the Old City of Jerusalem exhibits Christian icons and paintings, antiques and religious objects.

89 • The image shows some buildings in the classic white Jerusalem stone.

90 • The Christian faithful flood the Via Dolorosa during the Good Friday procession.

90-91 • A large number of pilgrims participating in the celebration of Palm Sunday, which commemorates the triumphal entry of Jesus into the holy city.

92 • His Beatitude Fouad Twal, Latin Patriarch of Jerusalem (in the foreground, dressed in purple and white), guides, with the help of some prelates, the procession of Palm Sunday.

93 • Representatives of the Catholic clergy, dressed in their white robes, parade around the Stone of Unction in the Basilica of the Holy Sepulchre, holding lighted candles.

On Mount Zion, just outside the walls erected by Suleiman the Magnificent, stands the Church of the Dormition, a place revered by Christians in memory of the Mother of Jesus Christ.

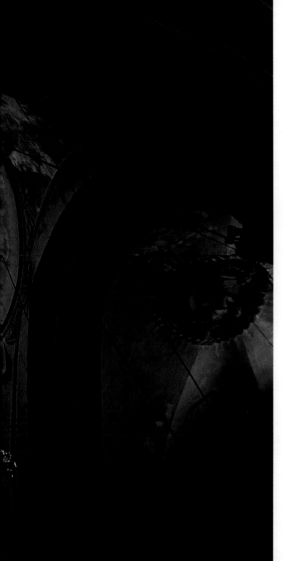

96-97 ● A dome with twisted ribs, typical of many Armenian churches, also adorns the Armenian Orthodox Cathedral of St. James the Great, consecrated to James the apostle, who was beheaded in Jerusalem in 44 AD.

97 ● Under the main altar of the church is the tomb of the first bishop of Jerusalem, over whose house the cathedral was built.

לעילוי נשמת

בר יעקב כהן

המנוחה שרה בר שלום חיון נדבת משפחת כהן־חיון

דוד טל ישראל חי יקום

98-99 • This tomb of uncertain date, covered by a black cloth, according to Jewish tradition would be the Tomb of King David, and as such it is revered.

99 • Even this colonnade conceals one of the holiest places in Jerusalem, which in this case is dear to Christians: it is, in fact, where Jesus ate the Last Supper with his disciples.

100-101 ● These ancient stone arches offer fascinating glimpses into a street in the Armenian Quarter.

101 ● From the walls of the citadel you can catch a glimpse of the Omar Ibn El-Khattab square, a point of passage for pilgrims and the religious.

102 • This glimpse of a street in the Jewish quarter of Jerusalem captures all the wealth of imagery and atmosphere that surrounds you in the old town.

103 • Children playing near the columns of the *cardo maximus*, which dates back to Roman times.

104-105 ● This covered road in the Jewish quarter follows the same path as the ancient Roman *cardo*.

105 ● Some of the buildings of the Jewish quarter stand out for the purity of white stone with which they are built.

106 ● The classic buildings of Jerusalem, of sober and square design, are the backdrop to the games of a group of girls.

107 ● A grandfather and Orthodox Jew is portrayed in a quiet moment in the company of his grandson.

On the rooftops of Jerusalem you will see water tanks, antennas and minarets, in a continuous contrast between ancient and modern, sacred symbols and objects of everyday life.

110-111 • A noisy and colorful Arab market greets visitors just inside the Damascus Gate.

111 • The white stone minarets are symbols of Muslim Jerusalem.

112 • A cyclist – an Orthodox Jew, judging from his clothing – winds up in an alley in the old town.

113 • This elderly Arab baker shows satisfaction with the abundance of goods displayed on the counter of his shop, including classic forms of bread with sesame seeds.

114-115 ● This shop for clothes, antiques and jewelry has been created under the vaulted cellars of the old city.

115 ● A head covering for Muslim women is the veil, sold in a variety of patterns and colors.

116 • In the covered section of the Arab souk, the comings and goings of customers and retailers are less intense than those that characterize the commercial areas outside the city.

117 • Wooden decorations and stained glass windows decorate a historical spot of the grand entrace in the old Arab quarter of the city, where men of various ages play cards.

Bargaining, Middle East style,
is now a must for the dealers
and buyers of Jerusalem.

Jewelry, colorful rugs and pans filled with colorful spices hang everywhere in the markets: you fish out the spices you want with a wooden spoon instead of buying prepackaged and aseptic products. Even this is part of Jerusalem's special appeal.

● The hill of
Gethsemane, facing
the temple's esplanade.
In the time of Jesus, the
skyline of Jerusalem
was not very different.

124-125 • The dome of the
Sanctuary of Dominus Flevit, on
the Mount of Olives, is the work
of Italian architect Antonio Barluzzi.

125 • These olive trees in the
Garden of Gethsemane are
probably thousands of years old.

126 ● Rocks are deposited as a sign of remembrance on a Jewish grave on the Mount of Olives.

126-127 ● It is in the Jehoshaphat Valley, near Gethsemane, where the Final Judgment is predicted to take place. Many believers are buried here.

In the Kidron Valley, next to Gethsemane, you will find the tombs of Zechariah and Absalom, monumental burial sites from the 1st or 2nd century.

130 ● This modern building is influenced by the Jerusalem style.

131 ● At the intersection of a street in the northern part of the new city of Jerusalem stands this impressive complex of buildings.

132-133 • Safra Square is the
town hall square of the new city.
In this image you can see an
outdoor modern art exhibition.

133 • The Hebrew University
building is lined with the traditional
white stone of Jerusalem.

134 ● Ben Yehuda Street is one of the most characteristic pedestrian streets of modern Jerusalem.

134-135 ● Jaffa Road, one of the most important streets of the city, combines the old with modern bus stations and trains.

136-137 ● In the evening, windows and fountains light up the modern Mamilla Mall, a shopping center just a short walk from the Jaffa Gate.

137 ● An innovative and newly built complex, the Mall is a compromise between modernity and tradition.

138 • The windmill that lies just outside the Jaffa Gate was built in the 19th century
by the English philanthropist Joseph Montefiore.

139 • Over the last century, the modern city, with its large buildings and busy streets,
has grown alongside historical Jerusalem.

140 • The YMCA, the youth hostel in Jerusalem, is housed in a historic building dating back to 1933.

140-141 • Mount Scopus has always offered a unique vantage point. Used in the past as a military base, it now houses, among other things, the Hebrew University of Jerusalem.

142 • The Jewish market of Mahane Yehuda, with its stalls of vegetables, is one of the most beloved by the citizens of Jerusalem and tourists.

143 • A very common scene in the Jewish Quarter: young Jewish mothers bring their children for a walk.

The Israel Museum, founded in the 1960s, is the largest cultural institution in Israel. There more than 500,000 pieces – archaeological finds and works of art – are conserved.

Within the "Shrine of the Book," by the enormous amphora-shaped roof, ancient Hebrew manuscripts are preserved.

148 and 149 • Inside the museum of Yad Vashem, visitors find commemorative plaques in memory of Holocaust victims and a reconstruction of the street in a ghetto, with pavement, railings and lampposts.

150-151 • A composition of 600 images and testimonies of Holocaust victims covers the great vault of the "Hall of Names" by Yad Vashem.

The windows in the synagogue at the Hadassah University Medical Center were made by Marc Chagall. Each window represents a different tribe of Israel.

REDISCOVERED
LAND

● A camel caravan stops in front of the Damascus gate, recognized for its elegant battlements, which remain unchanged today.

INTRODUCTION Rediscovered Land

UNTIL THE EARLY 19TH CENTURY, THE HOLY LAND REMAINED A MYSTERY FOR THE WESTERN WORLD: MORE A VAGUE ABSTRACTION THAN A CONCRETE PLACE WITH KNOWN LANDSCAPES AND CUSTOMS. IT WAS ALMOST A MYTH, ONE TIED TO THE BIBLE AND EPIC CHIVALROUS POEMS. JERUSALEM HAS ALWAYS BEEN A DESTINATION COVETED BY MERCHANTS AND ADVENTURERS, AND ONLY A FEW COURAGEOUS TYPES DREAMT OF GOING TO THE UNTOUCHED BUT DANGEROUS LAND OF THE OTTOMANS. THIS STARTED TO CHANGE AT THE TURN OF THE 19TH CENTURY, THANKS TO DAVID ROBERTS, A SCOTTISH PAINTER AND LANDSCAPE ARTIST, WHO BEGAN THE UNDERTAKING OF A LIFETIME: TRAVELLING THROUGH EGYPT, PALESTINE AND JORDAN WITH THE AIM OF DOCUMENTING MAJESTIC ANCIENT RUINS AND PLACES OF BIBLICAL

INTRODUCTION Rediscovered Land

IMPORTANCE. BACK HOME, ROBERTS TURNED THE PICTURES AND SKETCHES HE'D ACCUMULATED DURING HIS LONG VOYAGE INTO MULTIYEAR (1842-49) LITHOGRAPH PRINTS DIVIDED INTO TWO MASTERFUL COLLECTIONS DEDICATED TO EGYPT AND THE HOLY LAND: COLLECTIONS THAT FOUND HUGE SUCCESS IN ENGLAND, AS WELL AS THE REST OF THE OLD CONTINENT.

THANKS TO THESE LITHOGRAPHS, THE HOLY LAND AND ITS INHABITANTS FINALLY HAD IMAGES THAT REPRESENTED THEM: CITIES, COSTUMES, LANDSCAPES AND ARCHAEOLOGICAL REMAINS. EUROPE DISCOVERED THE DOMES AND MINARETS OF JERUSALEM, THE RUGGED SINAI MOUNTAINS AND THE GENTLE JORDAN VALLEY. AND THE MIDDLE EAST, WITH ALL ITS RELIGIOUS AND EXOTIC CHARM, BEGAN TO ENTER THE IMAGINATION OF WRITERS AND ARTISTS.

INTRODUCTION Rediscovered Land

INDEED, THE HOLY LAND WOULD SOON BE VISITED BY THE RUSSIAN POET NIKOLAI GOGOL (1848), THE FRENCH NOVELIST GUSTAVE FLAUBERT (1850) AND THE AMERICAN AUTHOR MARK TWAIN (1867). ON MARCH 9, 1842, THE PREMIERE OF GIUSEPPE VERDI'S "NABUCCO" WAS STAGED AT LA SCALA IN MILAN. NOT BY CHANCE, THE OPERA WAS SET IN JERUSALEM AND PALESTINE AND ALONG THE EUPHRATES. BUT THE WEST'S AWAKENING TOWARDS THE EAST WAS NOT ONLY ARTISTIC; THE ATTENTION COMING FROM EUROPE AND THE REST OF THE WORLD WAS ALSO OF AN ECONOMIC NATURE: IN 1869, THE SUEZ CANAL OPENED IN EGYPT, AND IT HAS SINCE REVOLUTIONIZED THE GEOGRAPHY OF INTERNATIONAL COMMERCIAL TRAFFIC. FROM THAT POINT ON, THERE WAS NO NEED TO CIRCUMNAVIGATE AFRICA TO

INTRODUCTION Rediscovered Land

REACH INDIA. SHIPS, WITH BOTH GOODS AND PASSEN-GERS, WERE NOW HEADING TO THE MIDDLE EAST. THIS MULTIPLIED CONTACTS, TRAVEL AND KNOWLEDGE. TO CELEBRATE THE SUEZ CANAL, VERDI STAGED HIS MASTERLY OPERA, "AIDA", IN CAIRO IN 1871. EUROPEAN READERS, MEANWHILE, LEARNED ABOUT THE MOD-ERN-DAY MIDDLE EAST THROUGH POPULAR NOVELS: THE FIRST PAGES OF JULES VERNE'S FAMOUS "AROUND THE WORLD IN 80 DAYS" (1873) SAW ITS HEROES EM-BARKING IN CAIRO, FROM A SHIP THAT HAD COME FROM THE PORT OF BRINDISI. VISITING THE HOLY LAND, ONCE AN IMPOSSIBLE TASK, BECAME AN AFFORDABLE ADVENTURE TOUR. THIS IS HOW THE FIRST WAVE OF POPULAR TRAVEL BEGAN, WITH PILGRIMAGES TO PLACES OF WORSHIP.

160-161 • Some merchants travel the spice route as the sun rises over the Gulf of Aqaba at the Red Sea. Not far from the coast, the island of Graia rises, topped by a Muslim fortress.

162-163 • On the terrace in front of the church of St. Anne, pilgrims pray. In the background, the dome of the Mosque of Omar stands on the ruins of the holy city.

The so-called "Tower of David" above the fortifications of the citadel, with its surrounding massive walls and deep moat.

Citadel of Jerusalem, called the Tower of David

Golden Gate of the Tem
Jerusalem

166-167 • Already at the time of David Roberts, many people were buried in front of the Golden Gate, through which – according to the prophecy – the Messiah will have to pass on his return to the city.

167 • A group of men converse at the ruins of the citadel at the northwestern corner of Jerusalem's Western Hill.

Church of the Holy Sepulchre
Jerusalem

168-169 • A scene from daily life:
with the background of the
crumbling facade of the
Romanesque Basilica of the
Holy Sepulchre, locals smoke
long pipes.

169 • Inside the basilica, we kneel
in front of the Stone of Unction,
on which, according to tradition,
Christ's body was laid.

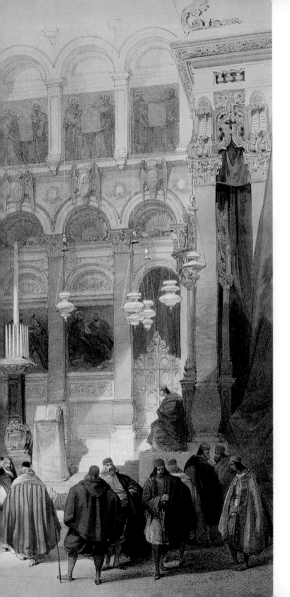

170-171 • Some pilgrims pray in the Katholikon, regarded by Orthodox Christians as the heart of the Holy Sepulchre.

171 • The shrine of the Holy Sepulchre, topped with two large drapes. It looked much the same in the 19th century.

● This view of the
landscape of eastern
Jerusalem has been
created by a vantage point
located south of the city
across the Kidron Valley.
On the right, clearly visible,
are the tomb of Zechariah,
that of Bene Hezir (also
known as the tomb
of St. James), and
that of Absalom, with
the typical roof.

174 • In this lively and animated scene depicting an encampment of pilgrims, dominated by the governor's tent, we see, in the background, the flat surface of the Dead Sea and to the right, galloping horsemen.

174-175 • The pilgrims bathe in the river of John the Baptist. Their stage is the Transjordan hills, with their magnificent landscapes.

Banks of the J...

David Roberts. R.A.

Nil 2nd 1839.

Convent of St. Saba. April 4th 1839

Louis Haghe, R.A.

Perched on steep cliffs in a canyon carved by the Kidron, the majestic Greek Orthodox monastery of Mar Saba stands. Roberts likely came from the city of Bethlehem after a long journey.

178 • The old Convent of the Holy Land in the village of Nazareth is immersed in the countryside of Galilee and surrounded by rolling hills.

178-179 • This was how the altar of the Franciscan Church of the Annunciation in Nazareth (later replaced by a larger, modern church) appeared when David Roberts visited it in April 1839.

● Some travelers take a break in front of Acre. The white city skyline stands out against the blue of the Mediterranean.

The ROOTS of the PAST

- The fortress of Masada, built by Herod the Great and pillaged by the Roman legions after a grueling siege, dominates the surrounding area.

INTRODUCTION The Roots of the Past

IN THE NEAR EAST, THOUSANDS OF YEARS AGO, A LAND BLESSED BY GOD FOR THE RICHNESS OF ITS SOIL, MILD CLIMATE AND GREAT CIVILIZATIONS, FLOURISHED. AT ITS HEART WAS SOMETHING CALLED THE "FERTILE CRESCENT": AN INVERTED CRESCENT THAT POINTED TO EGYPT AND PALESTINE IN THE WEST, AND THE MOUTH OF THE TIGRIS AND EUPHRATES RIVERS IN THE EAST. TO THE NORTH, LIED THE BIG BELLY OF MESOPOTAMIA, WHICH COVERED THE TERRITORIES OF PRESENT-DAY SYRIA AND IRAQ. OVER THE CENTURIES, FORESTS AND FIELDS DISAPPEARED AND THE DESERT ADVANCED. GREAT CITIES MENTIONED IN THE BIBLE WERE ABANDONED. BUT SIGNS OF ITS ANCIENT SPLEN-DOR, ARCHAEOLOGICAL FINDS OF IMMEASURABLE VALUE, ARE STILL THERE, WHICH MAKES THIS REGION ONE OF THE MOST INCREDIBLE OPEN-AIR MUSEUMS IN THE WORLD. IN THE NORTH-

This star-shaped window was found at Jericho in the ruins of the Palace of Hisham, the Umayyad architectural marvel.

INTRODUCTION The Roots of the Past

EAST OF SYRIA, FOR EXAMPLE, YOU CAN FIND (ALBEIT IN RU-
INS) MARI: A ONCE POWERFUL MESOPOTAMIAN CITY FROM
4,000 YEARS AGO. ON THE SYRIAN COAST OF THE MEDITER-
RANEAN, EXCAVATIONS HAVE UNEARTHED UGARIT, A CITY
FROM 5,000 YEARS AGO. THE OLDEST KNOWN EVIDENCE
OF THE USE OF AN ALPHABET ARE IN THE THOUSANDS OF
CLAY TABLETS FOUND IN THEIR ARCHIVES. IN THE SYRIAN
DESERT, MEANWHILE, LIES PALMYRA: THE CITY HAD ITS
PEAK IN THE 3RD CENTURY BC. ITS WONDERFULLY PRE-
SERVED REMAINS COVER 50 ACRES, AND THE GREAT TEM-
PLE THAT DOMINATES IT IS DEDICATED TO BAAL, THE PA-
GAN GOD THE GREAT PROPHETS OF THE BIBLE RAILED
AGAINST. IN PALESTINE, THE ARCHAEOLOGICAL SITE OF
MAJOR INTEREST IS NO DOUBT JERICHO, THE ONLY CITY IN
THE WORLD THAT CAN BOAST 10,000 YEARS OF UNBRO-
KEN HISTORY. THE OASIS OF JERICHO WAS A WELCOME

INTRODUCTION The Roots of the Past

RETREAT FOR MEN AS EARLY AS THE PROTO-NEOLITHIC (8000 BC) AND NEOLITHIC (6000 BC) PERIODS. THE REMNANTS OF DEFENSIVE WALLS OF THE BRONZE AGE (3000 BC) COULD BE THE REMAINS OF THE LEGENDARY WALLS OF JERICHO, WHICH JOSHUA TOPPLED WITH THE SOUND OF TRUMPETS. THE RUINS OF HEROD'S PALACE AND THE MAGNIFICENT MOSAICS OF THE UMAYYAD PALACE, MAKE IT A UNIVERSAL SITE, CHERISHED BY ALL PEOPLE OF THE HOLY LAND. HALF WAY BETWEEN THE DEAD SEA AND RED SEA, IN JORDINIAN TERRITORY AND ON THE ANCIENT STREET OF SPICE MERCHANTS, IN THE MOUNTAINOUS REGION OF EDOM, YOU'LL FIND THE AMAZING PETRA, CAPITAL OF THE NABATAEANS, A BEAUTIFUL AND VITAL CITY FROM THE 1ST CENTURY BC. ACCESSIBLE ONLY THROUGH A 1 MILE LONG CANYON, AFTER YOU'VE CROSSED IT, THE CITY CARVED INTO ROCK WILL SPRING TO LIFE IN FRONT OF

The Roots of the Past

Introduction

YOUR EYES AND LEAVE YOU SPEECHLESS. THE HOLY LAND, THE CRADLE OF PEACE, IS ALSO THE SCENE OF BLOOD AND CONFLICT. HIGH ABOVE THE HOLY LAND TOWER THE RUINS OF MAGNIFICENT CASTLES. A FEW MILES FROM THE DEAD SEA, PERCHED ON A HUGE SUNNY CLIFF, MASADA DOMINATES THE SCENERY. WHEN THE ROMAN LEGIONS DESTROYED JERUSALEM IN THE 1ST CENTURY AD, IT WAS HERE THAT THE LAST DETERMINED JEWS SOUGHT REFUGE, HEROICALLY RESISTING THE SIEGE FOR ALMOST THREE YEARS. DURING THE CRUSADER PERIOD, THE HOLY LAND WAS DOTTED WITH CHRISTIAN CASTLES; THE SHAWBAK FORTRESS, OR MONTREAL KRAK, PERCHED ON JORDANIAN SOIL, WAS IN THE MIDDLE AGES THE LAST BASTION OF THE WESTERN WORLD. OVERLOOKING THE DESERT, IT WAS THE EPIC BACKDROP OF SIEGES AND BATTLES BETWEEN CHRISTIANS AND MUSLIMS.

- Sepphoris, in Galilee, was a rich Roman town in the 1st century. In this period, mosaics of beautiful workmanship appeared; this female head is an example.

190-191 • Of the Nimrod Fortress, built by Muslims to protect Damascus, only ruins remain.

192 • The Byzantine mosaic with a basket of loaves and two fishes, in memory of the miraculous multiplication of Jesus, is at Tabgha on Lake Galilee.

192-193 • The synagogue at Capernaum, in the town of San Pietro, now looks like this. The ruins correspond to a building from the 4th century AD.

194-195 ● A large mosaic of the zodiac signs dominates the floor of the ancient synagogue of Hammath.

195 ● The same mosaic depicts a number of Jewish ritual objects, including a seven-branched menorah.

196-197 • Despite the destruction suffered, the perfect geometry of the Crusader fortress of Belvoir, south of Lake Galilee, is still admired.

197 • The Crusader castle is now roof-free, as we see in this open air room.

198-199 • Dating from the 1st century BC, the Roman theater dominates the old town of Beit She'an, the rich capital of the Decapolis.

200-201 • The remains of the elegant columns are an eloquent sign of the power of the town of Beit She'an in Roman times.

202 • Beit She'arim with its necropolis has resurfaced recently thanks to some excavations.

202-203 • The Tell Megiddo, or Mountain of Megiddo, inhabited for thousands of years until the 6th century BC, offers a vast variety of archaeological finds.

204-205 ● The large diameter of the load-bearing pillars and the amplitude of the basement vaults of Acre amaze the visitor.

205 ● In this hall of the castle, high ceilings provide better air circulation, which is essential in a warm climate like that of the Holy Land.

● The monumental remains of the Roman aqueduct in Caesarea testify to extraordinary engineering work, which brought water to the city from the slopes of Mount Carmel.

208 • A trading port famous since ancient times, Caesarea owes its splendor to King Herod, who beautified it in the 1st century BC.

208-209 • At the wonderful Roman Amphitheatre, the background is the horizon. Even today this beautiful space is used for shows and performances.

210 ● This wing of the fortified city built by the crusaders in the coastal city of Caesarea Maritima is still standing and visitable after 800 years.

211 ● Solid vaults greet visitors at the entrance of the city from the Crusader period of Caesarea Maritima.

● In spite of the damage that time and history have done to the city, you can still cross the elegant arches built by the Crusaders in Caesarea more than seven centuries ago.

● The enigmatic face
of a large statue is lit
by the sunset near
Mitzpe Ramon in the
Negev desert.

216-217 ● Palace of Hisham in Jericho is characterized by an imposing colonnade; it was built in the 8th century AD during the Umayyad dynasty.

217 ● Much of the charm of this building lies in its perfect perspectives.

218-219 ● In Beit Guvrin you can find frescoes in a tomb carved in the rock, dating back at least to the 2nd century BC.

220 • Herodion, the hill with the ruins of the famous palace of Herod the Great,
recalls the mouth of a volcano.

221 • Four large circular towers complete the massive structure of the fortress,
built for defensive purposes but also for appearance's sake, as it was the royal residence.

222 • The remains of the huge winter palace of Herod, a building overlooking the city of Jericho at the time of Jesus, are unfortunately in a state of abandonment.

222-223 • On the hillside of Herodion, a recent archaeological campaign may have found the tomb of Herod the Great.

The fortress of Masada seems impregnable, clinging to the top of the mountain on which King Herod wanted to build an "eagle's nest" in the 1st century BC.

226 • The buildings inside the fortress of Masada have undergone extensive restoration. Interesting Roman frescoes have also been found.

226-227 • Remains of the thermal baths at Masada: the fortress, equipped with cisterns, stores and abundant stocks of cattle, withstood the siege for three years before falling.

Of the ancient Nabatean city of Avdat all that remains is the perimeter of the walls, which still dominate the view in the immensity of the Negev desert.

230-231 • A decoration with two lions adorns a building of Avdat, once the obligatory stop for the caravans journeying along the incense or spice routes.

231 • The pagan temples of Avdat in the Byzantine period were transformed into churches whose impressive colonnades still remain.

232-233 ● In the heart of the Negev desert rises Mamshit, the smallest and best-preserved of the ancient Nabatean cities.

233 ● The large mosaic in the Church of the Nile of Mamshit contains a long inscription in Greek.

234-235 • At Shivta, the Nabatean center of the Negev that thrived in the Byzantine era, you can find the remains of this stone building with two apses.

235 • Particularly impressive is the wall structure of the city, which UNESCO in 2005 declared a World Heritage Site, as part of the "Incense Route - Desert Cities in the Negev" itinerary.

236 • Elegant floor mosaics decorate the Nirim synagogue, which probably dates back to the 5th century AD.

236-237 • Near Be'er Sheva, a city mentioned in the Bible and in the story of Abraham, you can admire an archaeological *tell* of great interest.

● An impressive ring
of walls surrounds
the crusade fortress
of Shawbak, not far
from Petra in Jordan.

WATERS
of the
SPIRIT

• Rocks covered with white salt crystals emerge from the vapors of the Dead Sea, on the West Bank side of the great salt lake.

INTRODUCTION Waters of the Spirit

On the world map, the boundaries of the holy land are painted with blue ink. In the land of deserts and spirituality, in fact, it is the blue of water that has traced and contained the ancient story of Jews, Muslims and Christians.

If you look from the holy land to the west, the natural boundary is the blue horizon of the Mediterranean. From there came Roman ships, decorated with the threatening insignias of the empire that would destroy Jerusalem. Peter and Paul trod back along the same route to bring the gospel to the capital of the known world. And 1,000 years later, fleets of crusaders

- From the Sanctuary of Beatitudes, on a hill near Capernaum, there is a splendid view of Lake Tiberias.

INTRODUCTION Waters of the Spirit

NAVIGATED THE SAME MEDITERRANEAN WAVES TO END MUSLIM RULE OVER THE LAND TRODDEN BY CHRIST.

IF, HOWEVER, YOU TURN YOUR GAZE TO THE EAST, THE GEOLOGY OF THE RIFT VALLEY SIGNALS ANOTHER BLUE BORDER OF THE HOLY LAND. FROM NORTHERN SYRIA TO MOZAMBIQUE, THE PLANET IS MARKED BY A DEEP VERTICAL CUT: A 3,700 MILES LONG INLET, WITH VARIABLE DEPTH AND WIDTH, WHICH MILLIONS OF YEARS AGO CAUSED THE SEPARATION OF THE TEC-TONIC PLATES OF AFRICA AND ARABIA. THE RIFT VAL-LEY, IN ITS UPPER REACHES, IS THE HOLY LAND. IN THE NORTH, A VALLEY, WHICH, ACCORDING TO TRADITION, IS IN THE FORM OF A CITHER, WELCOMES THE SEA OF GALILEE, THE LARGE FRESHWATER LAKE THAT IS

INTRODUCTION Waters of the Spirit

DEEPLY CONNECTED TO THE STORY OF JESUS. IT WAS IN THE FISHING VILLAGES ON ITS BANKS WHERE THE MESSIAH PREACHED, ITS WATER HE WALKED ON, AND THERE WHERE THE STORM SUBSIDED. TODAY THE LAKE IS LIFE: IN A LAND OFTEN AFFECTED BY DROUGHT, ITS BASIN IS AN INDISPENSABLE RESERVOIR FOR IRRIGATION AND DRINKING WATER.

THE RIVER THAT PLUNGES INTO THE SEA OF GALILEE AND FLOWS OUT ALONG THE RIFT VALLEY TO THE SOUTH IS THE JORDAN. CONFINED POLITICALLY ALONG THE BORDERS BETWEEN THE KINGDOM OF JORDAN, IS-RAEL AND THE PALESTINIAN TERRITORIES, JORDAN IS, MORE THAN ANY OTHER RIVER, TIED UP IN THE HISTORY OF SALVATION. IT WAS IN CROSSING IT THAT THE

INTRODUCTION Waters of the Spirit

PEOPLE OF ISRAEL, AFTER 40 YEARS WANDERING IN THE DESERT, ENTERED THE PROMISED LAND. AND IT IS IN ITS WATERS THAT THE PROPHET JOHN BAPTIZED HIS COUSIN JESUS, WHO THEN BEGAN HIS PREACHING. THE JORDAN RIVER FINISHES ITS COURSE IN A LITTLE SALT SEA, UNIQUE IN THE WORLD. LOCATED AT THE LOWEST POINT OF DRY LAND, 1,388 FEET BELOW SEA LEVEL, THE DEAD SEA IS A PARADISE OF HEALTH TOURISM. SKIN DIS-EASES AND RESPIRATORY DISEASES ARE TREATED WITH ITS ABUNDANT SALTS; ITS MUD IS TURNED INTO CREAMS EXPORTED ALL OVER THE WORLD. ITS SALINE CONCRE-TIONS, MEANWHILE, ARE AMAZING SALT SCULPTURES ADMIRED BY VISITORS.

INTRODUCTION Waters of the Spirit

IN THE SOUTH, FINALLY, THE HOLY LAND IS AS WET AS A BLESSING FROM THE RED SEA. ITS WATERS, SAYS THE BIBLE, ARE THE WATERS OF THE GREAT PASSAGES: THE WAVES ONCE OPENED FOR THE PEOPLE LED BY MOSES, WHO, IN PASSING THROUGH THEM, WENT FROM SLAVERY TO FREEDOM, ESCAPING FROM THE PHARAOH. TODAY, HOWEVER, THESE ARE THE WATERS OF GREAT TOURISM: SHARM EL SHEIKH IN EGYPT, EILAT IN ISRAEL AND AQABA IN JORDAN ARE WELL-KNOW DESTINATIONS FOR FUN AND RELAXATION. MILLIONS OF TOURISTS OPT FOR THE STUNNING BACKDROPS, AN ABUNDANCE OF TROPICAL FISH AND THE YEARLONG HOT AND SUNNY CLIMATE.

248 • A white wall overlooking the Mediterranean Sea is lashed by its waves.

248-249 • For centuries, the sea has carved inlets and caves in the white chalk cliffs of Rosh Hanikra, a town on the northern coast of Israel on the border with Lebanon.

● This sculpture shaped like a hand on the beach in Herzliya, near Tel Aviv, seems to be telling the waves to stop.

252 ● The Israeli Mediterranean coast is dotted with crystal clear bays and coves.

252-253 ● The rugged Rosh Hanikra rocks emerge among the green of the Galilee and the blue Mediterranean Sea.

254-255 ● The great Caesarea beach is crossed by the ancient Roman aqueduct, still standing firmly.

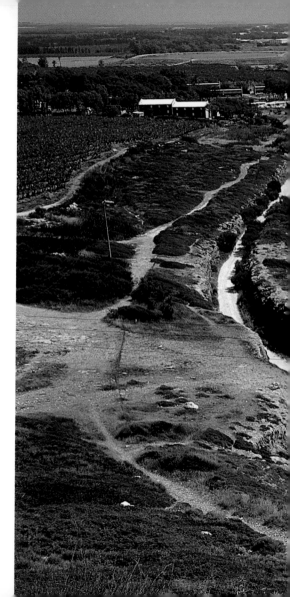

256 • Boats enjoy a sunny dock in the calm of a small bay.

257 • The river water flows into the sea, drawing plots of shapes and colors in the sand bed at the water's edge.

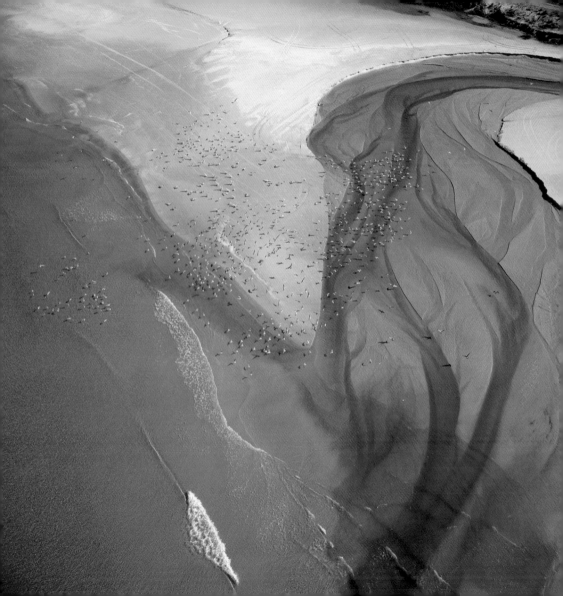

White sands, blue sea and an occasional bush are the ingredients of an unspoiled stretch of the Israeli Mediterranean coast.

Sdot Yam, one of the
first Israeli kibbutzim,
overlooks a clear water
bay not far from
Caesarea.

262 • A small waterfall on the Ayun
River in northern Israel flows into
a pool of water.

262-263 • In Banyas, on the border
with Lebanon, you will find the source
of the Jordan River. After a few miles
of slopes and cascades, the water
flows into the "Sea of Tiberias."

● Lake Hachula, in Upper Galilee, is the nature reserve many species of birds travel through in the course of their migrations.

266-267 ● In this picture of the archaeological excavations of Capernaum, an ancient fishing village on Lake Tiberias where Jesus lived, the large roof from the home of the apostle Peter is visible.

267 ● Around the Sea of Galilee there are many places of worship, including a purple-domed Orthodox church.

268 • The arid Negev desert seems far away: in Galilee, the lake offers all the water necessary for the fertile fields to bear fruit.

269 • The blue ribbon of the Jordan River travels nearly 10 miles before finally arriving and immersing itself in the waters of Lake Tiberias.

270 • The cultivated land around the lake draws a colorful checkerboard. The profile of the city of Tiberias overlooks the water.

271 • The coast where Jesus preached, in Capernaum and Bethsaida, can be glimpsed in the background.

272-273 • The Sea of Galilee, Israel's largest freshwater lake, is considered a large natural sanctuary. Over the centuries, in fact, man has built very little around the lake, and today it looks much the same as it did in the time of Jesus.

The abundance of water
and the industriousness of
man have made the land
near the lake one of the
most fertile and productive
sites throughout
the Holy Land.

276-277 • Without the Jordan River, the valley shared by Jordan and Israel would not have its proverbial fertility.

278-279 • Near the Dead Sea is the mountain range of Sodom, including the city the Bible says God destroyed because of its sins.

280-281 ● Reflections on the waters of the Dead Sea, in the region of the ancient city of Sodom, multiply the colors of the sky, the clouds and the rocky desert.

282-283 ● Ein Bokek is a famous tourist center on the Israeli side of the Dead Sea: beach umbrellas, deck chairs and water add comfort to the experience of immersing yourself in the salt lake.

284-285 • The evaporation of water lets archipelagos of salt concretions emerge on the shores of the Dead Sea.

285 • Creating a wonderful contrast of color, a saltwater canal cuts through an area completely devoid of vegetation.

286 ● In its southern area, the Dead Sea is an ordered sequence of ponds separated by long parallel banks.

287 ● As in a play of color, the earthy rock gives way to gray asphalt, the white of the waves and the green of the salt water.

288-289 ● The wealth of mineral crystals produces an unusual effect on a stretch of the coast of the Dead Sea.

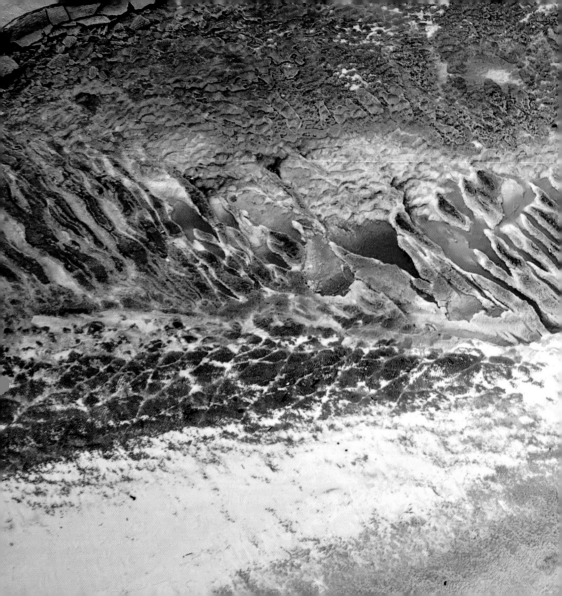

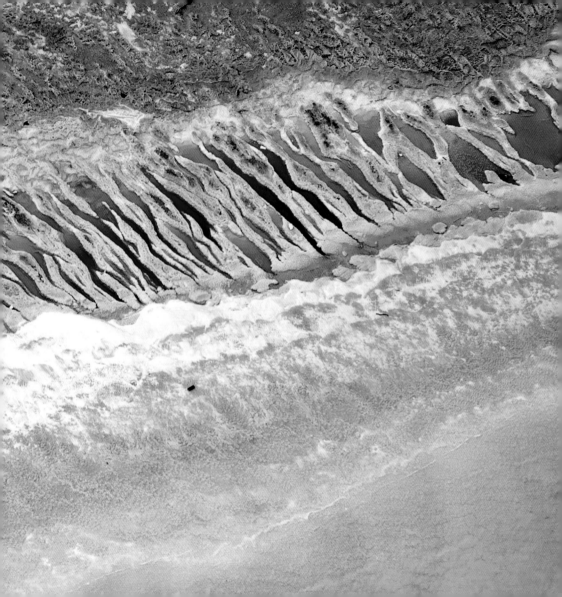

Sailboats and commercial ships flock to the Gulf of Aqaba, on the Red Sea, a tourist paradise shared by Israel and Jordan.

292 • The underwater observatory in Eilat has the shape of a spaceship. It allows even less experienced divers to enjoy the natural beauty of the Red Sea.

292-293 • During the visit to the observatory, after crossing a wooden bridge, you can board a real submarine to go down to the depths among fish and colorful coral.

294 • Gazing through the large window overlooking the underwater observatory in Eilat, you can find yourself face to face with tropical marine life.

295 • Two clown fish swim near a quiet sea anemone.

296 • A ray of sunshine lights up two dolphins, a mother with her baby, swimming
in shallow waters.

297 • A diver observes a dense flock of bewildered glass fish wrapped in the embrace
of two fierce lion fish.

● Close to the Egyptian coast of Sinai, on the Red Sea, a so-called "Pharaoh's Island" emerges from the water surmounted by a medieval fortress.

The SAND of the PROPHETS

- This huge stone mushroom is one of the natural wonders of Timna Park in the Negev desert in Israel.

INTRODUCTION The Sand of the Prophets

THE HOLY LAND IS AS VITAL AS WATER AND AIR, BUT ALSO SIMILAR TO SALT: WITHOUT IT, WE WOULD LOSE A LOT OF FLAVOR. MADE OF SILENCE AND WIND, THE HOLY LAND IS A SERIES OF MYSTERIOUS HORIZONS. IT'S THE DESERT, THE MAGICAL LANDSCAPE IN WHICH EVERYTHING HAS PLAYED AND CONTINUES TO HAPPEN: THE LARGEST RELIGIOUS EXPERIENCES, THE HISTORY OF BLOODY BATTLES BETWEEN THE MUSLIM EAST AND THE CHRISTIAN WEST, THE MIRACLE OF A NATURAL PARADISE STILL LARGELY UNTOUCHED.

THE VERY SOUL OF THE PEOPLE OF ISRAEL IS ROOTED IN THE DESERT: BE'ER SHEVA IS A MODERN CITY THAT LOOKS OUT ON THE ARIDITY OF NEGEV. RIGHT HERE,

Not far from Bethlehem, embedded in the wall of a deep and inhospitable wadi, the ancient monastery of Mar Saba rises.

INTRODUCTION The Sand of the Prophets

JUST UNDER 4,000 YEARS AGO, THE CARAVAN OF ABRAHAM PASSED, GUIDED ONLY BY THE PROMISE OF INFINITE DESCENT. AND IN THE SINAI DESERT RISE THE JORDANIAN MOUNTAINS, WHERE MOSES, FLEEING FROM EGYPT, LED HIS PEOPLE FOR 40 YEARS.

ABOVE THE OASIS OF JERICHO, SET IN THE RUGGED WALLS OF A MOUNTAIN AT THE EDGE OF THE JUDEAN DESERT, IS THE MONASTERY OF QUARANTINE, BUILT ON THE SITE WHERE JESUS, AFTER HIS BAPTISM, WAS LED BY THE SPIRIT TO PRAY AND BE TEMPTED. THE MAJESTIC SCENERY OF WADI KELT, ON THE ROAD FROM JERUSALEM TO JERICHO, HAS FOR CENTURIES HOSTED HUNDREDS OF CHRISTIAN MONKS IN ITS CAVES. EVEN TODAY, IN THE WADI, YOU CAN VISIT THE ORTHODOX MONASTERY OF ST. GEORGE OF KOZIBA. NOT FAR FROM

INTRODUCTION The Sand of the Prophets

BETHLEHEM STANDS THE IMPOSING MONASTERY OF MAR SABA. AT ONE TIME IT COULD ACCOMMODATE UP TO 4,000 MEN. MEANWHILE AT THE FOOT OF MOUNT SINAI IN EGYPT, YOU CAN FIND THE OLDEST CHRISTIAN MONASTERY, DEDICATED TO ST. CATHERINE AND ERECTED IN THE 4TH CENTURY AD AT THE PLACE WHERE GOD SPOKE TO MOSES FROM A BURNING BUSH. THE DESERT PROVIDES A PROFOUND EXPERIENCE OF SILENCE AND STILLNESS. VISITORS OFTEN FEEL THEY ARE ONLY A STEP AWAY FROM THE ETERNAL. DAWN AFTER DAWN, IT MAY SEEM THAT NOTHING CHANGES OR MOVES. THE VESTIGES OF HISTORY, IN THIS INFINITE STILLNESS, CAN SAFELY LAST MILLENNIA.

THIS IS WHAT HAPPENED WITH THE 30,000 PRECIOUS GRAPHITE ROCKS IN WADI RUM, WHICH DATE BACK

The Sand of the Prophets

Introduction

8,000 YEARS. THEY ARE THE MEMORY OF A TIME LONG AGO, WHEN THE IMMENSE JORDANIAN DESERT WAS IN-HABITED AND FERTILE. THE SAME THING HAPPENED AT QUMRAN, IN THE INACCESSIBLE CAVES ON THE ROCKY SHORES OF THE DEAD SEA. HERE, BY CHANCE, IN THE MIDDLE OF THE LAST CENTURY, A SHEPHERD FOUND PITCHERS FROM THE TIME OF CHRIST LYING IN THE DEPTHS OF A CAVE. INSIDE THEM WERE INVALUABLE, FRAGILE SCROLLS OF THE BIBLE.

BUT THE SEEMINGLY INFINITE DESERT IN THE HOLY LAND IS ALSO MOSTLY UNSPOILED NATURE. THE HUGE CRATER NEAR THE TOWN OF MITZPE RAMON, IN THE PARK OF THE NEGEV IN ISRAEL, IS ONE OF THE GEO-LOGICAL WONDERS OF THE WORLD.

Like a reef emerging from a sea of sand, a large rock formation at Wadi Rum, in Jordan, appears in all its grandeur.

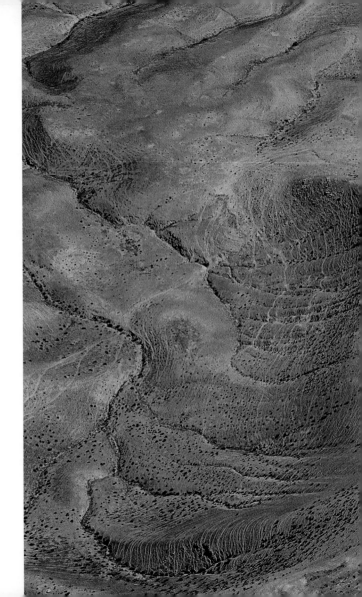

● The almost lunar landscape of the Judean desert in the West Bank: arid hills as far as the eye can see, punctuated only by small shrubs.

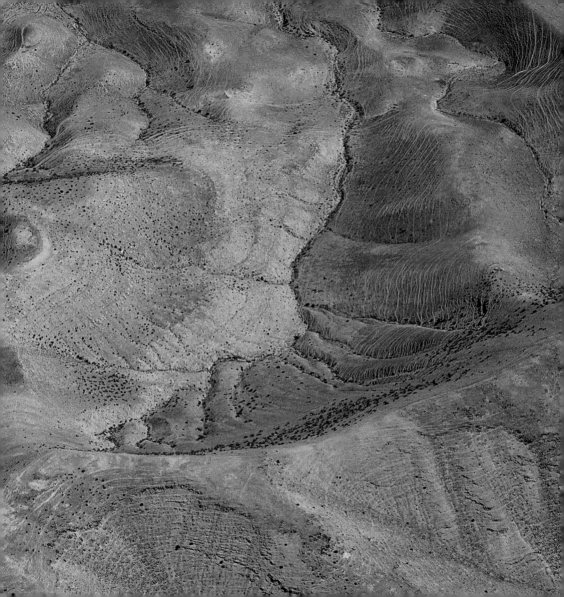

On a difficult-to-access rock over Jericho, the monastery of Quarantine stands, built where Jesus, after fasting for 40 days, was tempted by the devil.

312 • In the famous caves of Qumran, a few dozen years ago, a pastor by chance discovered ancient scrolls with texts from the Bible hidden in pots.

312-313 • As shown by recent excavations, in the 1st century AD Qumran was a thriving community of Essenes, observant Jews who practiced a monastic lifestyle.

● Like a fortress (and supported by massive buttresses), the mountain range where you can find the caves of Qumran.

The Orthodox monastery of St. George of Koziba, in the inacessible Wadi Kelt, above the city of Jericho, is still inhabited by religious practitioners.

318-319 ● In this rugged mountainous
area of the Negev, different kinds
of desert rock formations overlap.

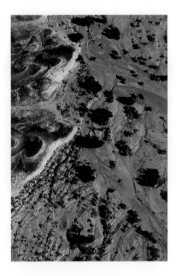

319 ● Small shrubs able to survive
without water are the only form
of plant life that can withstand the
aridity of the desert.

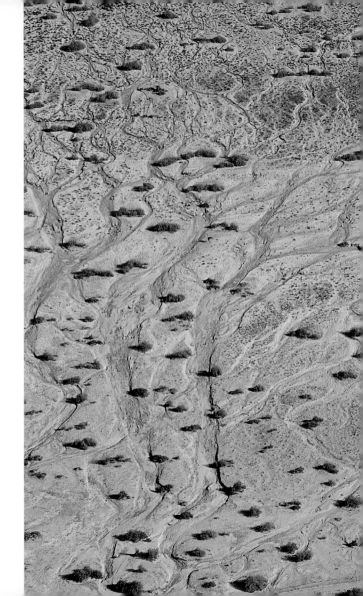

Shrubs, small sandy
channels and islands
of parched brown earth
decorated with the shapes
and colors of the desert's
vastness.

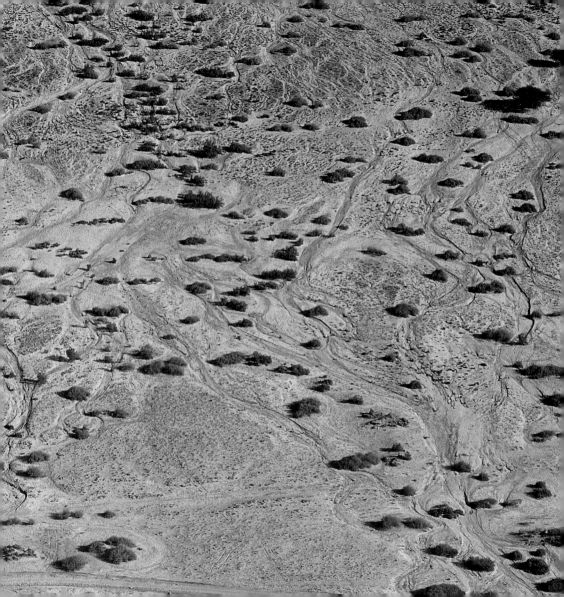

The profile of the huge crater near the town of Mitzpe Ramon is one of the geological wonders of Israel.

● A young Nubian ibex dominates the scene, faced with an impervious natural balcony overlooking the boundless basin of the Makhtesh Ramon.

● Hundreds of millions
of years ago, this area
was covered by the
ocean. The movement
of this water caused
the formation of the
great Ramon Crater,
24 miles long and
6 miles wide.

328 • Despite the unbearable heat of the Negev, lush flora grows at the bottom of the Ein Avdat canyon, thanks to the water.

329 • In the nature reserve of Ein Avdat, small and large waterfalls flow, their spray collected in pools of water carved into the rock.

● These huge rock
formations are known
as the "pillars of King
Solomon." They have been
shaped by wind and water
for thousands of years
in the nature reserve
of Timna.

● At Timna, the force
of nature and not the
hand of man has
shaped this "pyramid"
of stone, its overlapping
geological layers
eroding in a uniform
manner.

This magnificent stone arch was carved by the patient erosion of natural agents over thousands of years. It is one of the wonders that await you at Timna.

336-337 • The sandstone mountains of the Wadi Rum National Park in Jordan emerged 30 million years ago, following the movement that created the Rift Valley fault.

337 • In the silence of the desert, and with thousands of years of patient work, the imagination of nature has carved unusual shapes in the rock.

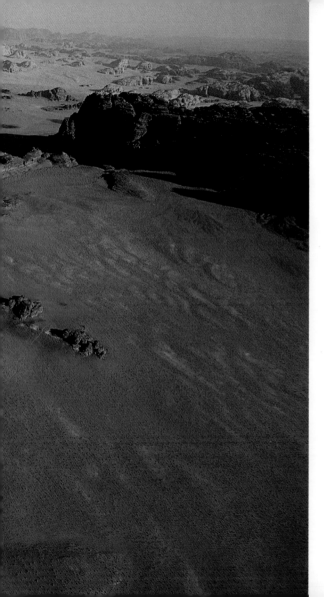

338-339 ● Thomas
Edward Lawrence,
better known as
"Lawrence of Arabia,"
intensely loved
Wadi Rum, describing
it as "vast, echoing
like a deity."

340-341 ● Desert
stone, but also the
sand: the solidity of
the sandstone cliffs
is associated with the
volatility of the dunes.
Wadi Rum owes its
appeal partly to this
double nature.

● An embroidery of thousands of windows, mullions and natural arches is the wonderful imprint left by the creation of this sandstone wall.

344 • Walls as high as 1,300 feet, to attack and beat in the silence of the desert, are a paradise for climbers who visit the Wadi Rum.

345 • The sun and wind draw small waves in a sea of red sand, from which a small shrub emerges.

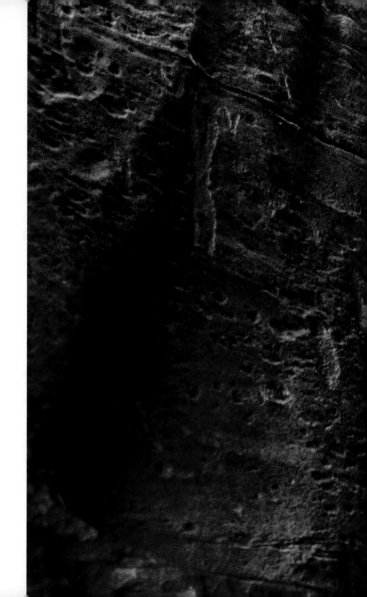

● Men and Nubian ibex engaged in ancient hunting scenes: this is one of more than 30,000 petroglyphs preserved on the soft sandstone walls of Wadi Rum.

348-349 • Thousands of tourists who annually visit the Wadi Rum spend at least one night in the desert in tent encampments like this one.

349 • The commercial railway, which transports precious cargo to the port of Aqaba, runs near Wadi Rum.

350-351 ● Near the Nabatean city of Petra in Jordan, a building dominates a desert promontory.

352-353 ● In all likelihood, caves carved into the walls of the headlands near the ancient city of Petra were used as burial sites.

● The mausoleum of Nabi Saleh, a wise man revered by many Muslims, can be found near St. Catherine's Monastery in Sinai.

356 • In a wall formed by large blocks of pale stone, a small door opens to St. Catherine's Monastery, perhaps the oldest in Christendom.

357 • The monastery was erected in the 4th century AD where Moses was surprised by the divine sign of the burning bush.

358 • Despite the arid surroundings, you can find cool air inside the monastery.

359 • Even today, a large religious community lives in St. Catherine's: several buildings inside the walls are used to accommodate its members.

360-361 • Near the top of Sinai, the so-called "Amphitheater of the Seventy Wise Men of Israel" stands. This is where the wise men of Israel waited for Moses to finish his dialogue with God.

361 • A lone shrub grows lush, its roots directly into the water tank of the Amphitheater of the Seventy Wise Men of Israel.

362 • To reach the shrine on Mount Sinai, you must walk for hours. Part of the route consists of a path of steps carved into the stone.

363 • The apse of a Greek Orthodox chapel built on top of Mount Sinai dominates its surroundings and emphasizes the immensity of the landscape.

364-365 • At sunset, the last light of day illuminates in red the peaks of the rough and evocative promontory of Sinai.

The cities between PAST and PRESENT

- To the north of the ancient port of Jaffa, as far as the eye can see, lies the forest of skyscrapers in Tel Aviv.

INTRODUCTION The Cities between Past and Present

IF YOU REALLY WANT TO EXPLORE THE HOLY LAND, TAKE TIME OUT TO VISIT ITS CITIES. THERE ARE THREADS THAT UNITE THEM ALL, VILLAGES AND URBAN CENTERS ALIKE: THE TRAFFIC JAMS, THE VITALITY OF THE SOUKS AND THE FRIENDLINESS OF THE PEOPLE. AT THE SAME TIME, HOWEVER, EACH IS UNIQUE.

DAMASCUS AND AMMAN ARE THE TWO MAJOR ARAB CAPITALS IN THE MIDDLE EAST. DAMASCUS IS THE CITY OF ST. PAUL'S CONVERSION. ITS OLD TOWN IS A JOURNEY BACK IN TIME, WITH THE SPLENDOR OF THE UMAYYAD MOSQUE AND THE REMAINS OF INDESTRUCTIBLE ROMAN ROADS. AROUND IT, A CROWDED METROPOLIS HAS GROWN OVER TIME, WITH A BREATHTAKING VIEW AT SUNSET FROM THE JEBEL QASSIOUN,

369 • The beaches of Tel Aviv are a traditional holiday resort for many Israelis.

374-375 • Acre, a stronghold for crusaders and then Muslims, is protected by UNESCO.

INTRODUCTION The Cities between Past and Present

THE HILL THAT DOMINATES THE CITY. AMMAN, ON THE OTHER HAND, WAS A SMALL VILLAGE AND A PILE OF ANCIENT RUINS. THIS CHANGED WHEN A RAILWAY LINE WAS BUILT, LINKING DAMASCUS AND MEDINA, FACILITATING THE PILGRIMAGE TO MECCA AND BENEFITING THE CITY'S DEVELOPMENT. FROM THAT POINT ON, AMMAN BEGAN TO GROW ALONG THE CLIFFS OF ITS 14 HILLS. TODAY, IT IS THE MODERN CAPITAL OF THE HASHEMITE KINGDOM OF JORDAN AND ALMOST HALF THE POPULATION OF THE STATE LIVES THERE.

BETHLEHEM AND NAZARETH, OF COURSE, ARE TWO OF THE MOST IMPORTANT CITIES OF THE CHRISTIAN TRADITION. THE FIRST, LOCATED IN PALESTINIAN TERRITORY, IS THE BIRTH-PLACE OF JESUS AND SITE OF THE OLDEST CHURCH IN THE HOLY LAND, VISITED BY MILLIONS OF PILGRIMS EVERY YEAR.

INTRODUCTION The Cities between Past and Present

THE SECOND, IN ISRAELI TERRITORY, IS THE CITY WHERE JE-
SUS LIVED FOR 30 YEARS. THERE, THE CAVE BELIEVED TO BE
THE HOME OF MARY IS VENERATED. THANKS TO A GREAT
LOCATION, NOT FAR FROM LAKE GALILEE, AND A LARGE IN-
FLUX OF PILGRIMS, NAZARETH HAS GROWN STEADILY OVER
THE YEARS.

SIMILAR AND YET VERY DIFFERENT, AMONG THEM ARE THREE
GREAT SEASIDE CITIES OVERLOOKING THE EASTERN COAST
OF THE MEDITERRANEAN: BEIRUT, TEL AVIV AND GAZA.

BEIRUT IS THE ARAB CAPITAL OF FINANCE AND ECONOMY:
LARGE BANKS HAVE THEIR HEADQUARTERS HERE AND MEM-
BERS OF THE ARAB ELITE GO THERE TO FIND A SHOPPING AND
HOLIDAY PARADISE. FOUNDED IN ANCIENT TIMES, IT OWES ITS
CHARM TO MORE RECENT HISTORY. BEIRUT IN THE 1940S

The Cities between Past and Present

Introduction

BECAME THE CAPITAL OF A MODERN MULTI-RELIGIOUS LEBANON, WHERE CHRISTIANS AND MUSLIMS LIVED TOGETHER. IN THE '60S, IT WAS KNOWN AS THE "PARIS OF THE MIDDLE EAST." BUT FROM 1975 TO 1990, IT WAS DEVASTATED BY CIVIL WAR, A CONSEQUENCE OF THE ARAB-ISRAELI CRISIS. AN IMPRESSIVE AMOUNT OF REBUILDING HAS, TODAY, BROUGHT IT BACK TO ITS PRE-WAR SPLENDOR. THE EFFECT, HOWEVER, IS BITTERSWEET: THE CENTER IS MODERN AND TECHNOLOGICALLY ADVANCED, WHILE IN THE SUBURBS YOU CAN STILL FIND PALESTINIAN REFUGEE CAMPS.

TEL AVIV HAS JUST CELEBRATED A CENTURY OF LIFE. AS A YOUNG CITY, IT HAS NEVERTHELESS BEEN DESIGNATED A UNESCO WORLD HERITAGE SITE FOR ITS BAUHAUS STYLE ARCHITECTURE. AS THE ECONOMIC AND FINANCIAL HEART OF

The Cities between Past and Present

Introduction

ISRAEL, IT IS THE ENGINE OF THE SECULAR OPPOSITION TO JERUSALEM, THE RELIGIOUS CAPITAL. WHEN IT COMES TO ART, MUSIC AND ENTERTAINMENT, TEL AVIV FINDS LITTLE TO ENVY IN NEW YORK, AND ITS INTERNATIONAL AIRPORT SEES MORE THAN 10 MILLION PASSENGERS A YEAR.

GAZA, FINALLY, IS THE MOST POPULOUS CITY OF THE PALESTINIAN TERRITORIES. DESPITE ITS FAVORABLE TRADE POSITION, IT DOES NOT BOAST THE WEALTH OF BEIRUT AND TEL AVIV DUE TO THE CLOSURE IMPOSED ON ITS OWN BORDERS. OVERLOOKING THE RED SEA IS A DIFFERENT SORT OF CITY: EILAT, A PARADISE FOR THOSE WHO LOVE THE SEA AND DIVING. IT IS THE ISRAELI CITY OF ENTERTAINMENT. EILAT HAS ALWAYS BEEN LOVED BY THE JEWISH PEOPLE, AND WAS EVEN MENTIONED IN THE BOOK OF EXODUS.

376 • The port of Akko (Acre) is now home to sailing boats and tourist ferries; once upon a time, crusaders sailed in from Europe.

377 • A mighty wall built by the Ottomans protects the citadel of Acre from the waves.

378 • The Church of St. John in the Old City of Akko was built on the site of a former medieval place of worship.

378-379 • The small white mosque of El-Jazzar, built within the Ottoman walls, is one of the most significant monuments of the old city of Akko.

380 • The front door of the white mosque of Akko is adorned with decorative circular marble of different colors.

381 • A large chandelier illuminates the interior of the mosque. In the background is the *mihrab*, the niche where the Imam leads the prayer.

382-383 • Observing Haifa from the the wonderful roof garden at the Bahá'í temple, a breathtaking view of the city reveals itself.

● Two modern
skyscrapers, with the
entire city of Haifa at
their feet, seem to scan
the endless horizon
of the Mediterranean.

386 • Haifa, with its port and commercial business district, is one of the major centers for the Israeli economy.

387 • The so-called "Sail Tower," a modern sail-shaped skyscraper, is one of the masterpieces of contemporary architecture in Haifa.

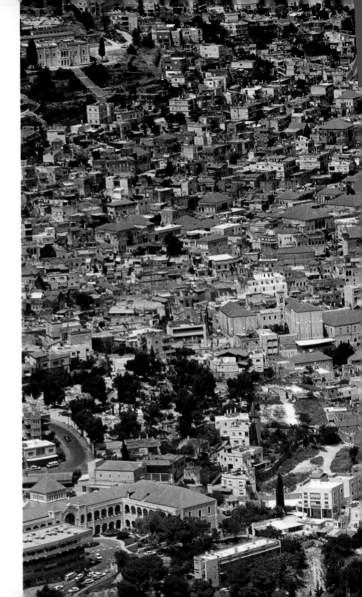

Nazareth, now a thriving Israeli town, has grown around its spiritual heart, the Basilica of the Annunciation.

390 • The cave around which the great basilica in Nazareth was built is believed to have been the home of Mary's family.

391 • Merchants offer their goods in the middle of a commercial street in the center of Nazareth.

392 • In this cave, according to Christian tradition, the angel Gabriel announced to Mary that she would become the mother of the Savior.

393 • The top of the Basilica of the Annunciation is an invitation to the faithful to look up to heaven.

394 ● The mosaic in the courtyard of the Basilica of Nazareth, among many others, was donated by Ukraine in honor of Mary.

395 ● The Christ Pantocrator, surrounded by angels and saints, adorns the golden vault of the Greek Orthodox Church of St. Gabriel in Nazareth.

396-397 ● Today Tiberias is a quiet tourist town overlooking the shores of the lake of the same name; at the time of Jesus, it was an important Roman port.

398-399 • Some swimmers enjoy a moment of relaxation on the beach in Jaffa, opposite the old port city.

399 • Jaffa has been known since ancient times: the cedars of Lebanon, necessary for the construction of Solomon's temple, came from here.

In the Middle Ages, on the docks of the port of Jaffa, many Christian pilgrims disembarked from ships that often came from Venice.

402 • The old town of Jaffa, with its narrow cobbled streets, is reminiscent of many historic centers in Italian cities.

402-403 • In Tel Aviv, an old stone arch frames a door with a golden cross.

404-405 ● Great beaches and luxurious hotels: the Tel Aviv seafront looks similar to many tourist cities in the West.

406-407 ● Yachts and sailing boats in a reserved port on the promenade overlooking the center of the Israeli metropolis.

• In the city center you can see some Bauhaus buildings. This is the style of architecture for which Tel Aviv has been recognized as a World Heritage Site by UNESCO.

410 • Like a wide placid river, this thoroughfare with many lanes crosses through the forest of buildings and skyscrapers of the metropolis.

411 • Large modern towers sprout suddenly like rock walls in the middle of residential neighborhoods in central Tel Aviv.

412 • The light of dawn illuminates the upper floors of the buildings in Tel Aviv and in the background, the indefinite blue of the Mediterranean Sea.

413 • The modern Hechal Yehuda synagogue in Tel Aviv, built thanks to donations from the Recanati family, resembles a seashell.

414 • An almost psychedelic night landscape with electric yellow, blue and violet lights at the exit of a road tunnel in the metropolis.

415 • City lights lay siege to the Sheraton in front of a beach in Tel Aviv. In the background, a forest of lit skyscrapers.

416 • The cloister of the Franciscan monastery, entrusted to the care of the Church of the Nativity in Bethlehem, is a place of peace.

417 • In this Christmas image, Bethlehem is covered with snow: perhaps the scenario in which Jesus was born, two thousand years ago, was similar.

418 • The central nave of the Basilica of the Nativity in Bethlehem is nearly 165 feet long and has looked like this for centuries.

419 • The main altar is adorned with lamps and chandeliers, silverware and icons, according to the style and tradition of the Eastern Church.

420 • Under the nave are the Grotto of the Nativity and the Grotto of the Manger, which see a constant influx of worshippers and visitors.

421 • In this precise location, marked by a silver star, Christian tradition marks the spot where Jesus came into the world.

The Grotto of the Nativity hosts continuous celebrations and rites from the rich variety of Eastern Christendom's Churches.

At the foot of the huge cliff in the Judean desert, before the natural border of Jordan, the green oasis of Jericho grows.

Jericho, among the most important Palestinian cities, is famous throughout the Middle East for its production of dates, fruit and citrus.

428 • Two women, standing near the ancient holy place of the iconostasis, admire the frescoes in the Monastery of the Quarantine.

428-429 • This monastery is almost camouflaged in the side of this mountain, which is only a few miles away from Jericho on foot.

● The tomb of Yasser Arafat, the Palestinian leader who died in 2004, is situated in this district, in the Muqata compound, in Ramallah, West Bank.

432 • The Palestinian town of Nablus lies at the foot of a hill in a countryside full of olive groves.

432-433 • A huge chandelier dominates the iconostasis of the Orthodox monastery of "Jacob's well" where Jesus met the Samaritan woman.

434-435 ● The large Muslim
complex remembered as the
"Tomb of the Patriarchs"
in Hebron is a religious site also
dear to Jews and Christians.

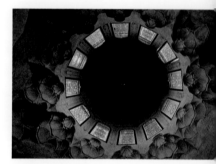

435 ● The vault of the Islamic
temple, Al-Haram al-Ibrahimi, also
known as the "Tomb of the
Patriarchs," is adorned with
12 stained glass windows.

436 • The Technical College of Be'er Sheva, the Israeli town of the Negev, has the unusual shape of a large inverted cylinder in glass and metal.

437 • Be'er Sheva has developed over the past 60 years with a focus on avant-garde architecture.

The Israeli city of Eilat and the nearby Jordanian city of Aqaba have grown thanks to the increased tourist pull of the Red Sea.

The PROMISED LAND

- Nahalan, among the first Jewish settlements founded in the last century, radiates like the sun in the green countryside of Galilee.

INTRODUCTION The Promised Land

IF THE PEOPLE OF THE MIDDLE EAST SHARE A DREAM, IT IS FOR A LAND OF "MILK AND HONEY", WHERE FRUIT GROWS ALMOST EFFORTLESSLY AND FOOD IS PLENTIFUL FOR HUMANS AND ANIMALS. FROM THE TIME OF ABRAHAM'S FATHER, GOD PROMISED THESE REWARDS IN THE BOOK OF GENESIS, SURPRISING A FRIGHTENED MOSES ON MOUNT SINAI WHILE THE FLOCK OF HIS STEP-FATHER, JETHRO, GRAZED.

DAVID WAS NOT A SOLDIER – THE BIBLE SAYS – WHEN HE WAS ANOINTED KING OF ISRAEL IN THE HILLS NEAR BETHLE-HEM. HE WAS JUST A YOUNG SHEPHERD, AND FOR THIS REASON, GOD CHOSE HIM. AND, IN THE NEW TESTAMENT, JESUS DESCRIBES GOD THE FATHER AS A "SOWER" WHO NEVER TIRES OF SOWING AND AS A "GOOD SHEPHERD" WHO

• The strange shape of this forest, surrounded by the lush hinterland areas of Israel, resembles the long strides of a runner.

INTRODUCTION The Promised Land

DOES NOT FORGET THE LAST OF HIS SHEEP. ALTHOUGH MOST OF THE WORK FORCE IS NOW ENGAGED IN INDUSTRY AND SERVICES, IN THE MIDDLE EAST AGRICULTURE AND SHEEP FARMING ARE STILL VERY POPULAR. TRANSHUMANCE IS PRACTICED IN SYRIA, IRAQ AND JORDAN, WHERE NOMADIC SHEPHERDS LEAD FLOCKS OF SHEEP AND CAMELS ON ROUTES THAT HAVE BEEN FOLLOWED FOR CENTURIES. BEFORE THE OCCUPATION AND CONFLICT BETWEEN ISRAEL AND PALESTINE, SHEEP FARMING WAS NOMADIC EVEN IN THE HOLY LAND: FLOCKS COULD BE SEEN GRAZING IN THE HILLS OF THE WEST BANK, BEFORE BEING BROUGHT TO THE JORDAN VALLEY IN THE WINTER. IT IS NO COINCIDENCE THAT THE BIRTH OF THE SAVIOR WAS ANNOUNCED TO SHEPHERDS, CAMPED NEAR BETHLEHEM IN THE SOUTH OF THE REGION.

INTRODUCTION The Promised Land

IN THE HOLY LAND, WATER FOR IRRIGATION IS MORE VALUABLE THAN OIL. RIVERS AND RESERVOIRS MUST BE CONSTANTLY HELPED BY THE RAIN, WHICH DOES NOT FALL OFTEN ENOUGH. THE EXCESSIVE EXPLOITATION OF THE JORDAN RIVER IN RECENT YEARS IS A CONCERN, AS IT RUNS THE RISK OF DRYING OUT. HOWEVER, IN PLACES RICH WITH IRRIGATION RESOURCES, THE FRUITS OF THE HOLY LAND ARE NOT INFERIOR TO THOSE PROMISED THOUSANDS OF YEARS AGO TO MOSES. ON THE BANKS OF THE MAJOR RIVERS (THE NILE, THE EUPHRATES AND THE JORDAN) THE INTENSE CULTIVATION CREATES COMPLEX MOSAICS OF COLORS; THE DIFFERENT SHADES OF GREEN AND BROWN FIELDS, CONTRAST WITH THE DESERT'S OCHER, WHICH VARIES IN INTENSITY. OLIVE TREES AND DATE PALMS ARE THE REGION'S MAINSTAYS,

The Promised Land

BUT GRAPEFRUIT, LEMONS AND OTHER CITRUS FRUITS ARE ALSO EXPORTED WORLDWIDE AND ARE THE REGION'S TASTIEST CALLING CARDS.

IN THE HOLY LAND, THANKS TO THE USE OF ADVANCED IRRIGATION TECHNOLOGIES, MAN HAS MIRACULOUSLY MADE THE DESERT BLOOM. IN THE LAST CENTURY IN ISRAEL, THE KIBBUTZ MOVEMENT HAS SPREAD, WITH COLLECTIVIST COMMUNITIES CHOOSING TO SET UP FARMS IN ARID REGIONS. AND, AS IF WISHING TO REITERATE THE DREAM OF FERTILE LAND THAT HAS NEVER FADED FOR THE JEWISH PEOPLE, DAVID BEN-GURION, THE FIRST PRESIDENT OF THE STATE OF ISRAEL, IS BURIED IN SDE BOKER, A DESERT KIBBUTZ.

- A field of olives in shades of green and brown colors the hills of Samaria, an arid tract which might otherwise not bear fruit.

With snow-capped peaks and slopes covered with forests, Mount Hermon recalls landscapes perhaps more common in Europe than in this land.

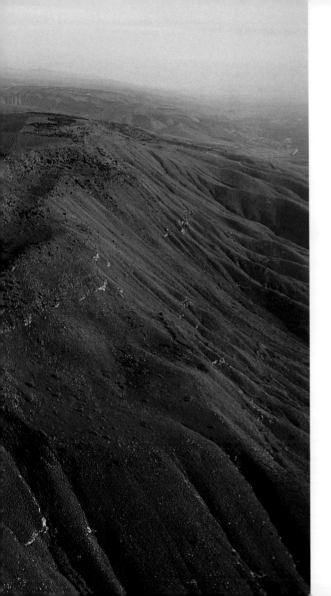

The Golan Heights, Syrian territory occupied by Israel in 1967 during the "Six Day War," are reserved mostly for grazing.

● Behind Metullah, an Israeli city near the border with Lebanon, you can see the snow-capped Mount Hermon.

454 • The landscape of the hills of Galilee, covered with green pastures and rare shrubs, inspires a sense of gentleness and harmony.

455 • In this plain between two hills in Hattin, Saladin defeated the Christian army in 1187, decreeing the end of the Crusader kingdom of Jerusalem.

456-457 ● On Mount Tabor, where there is a large church, Jesus was transfigured before some of his disciples, showing the splendor of his divinity.

458-459 ● The view from the summit of Mount Hermon, the natural border between Syria and Lebanon, is truly boundless.

460-461 ● Near Akko, Israel, in the middle of a garden decorated with plants and flowers, is an important site of the Bahá'í faith.

462-463 ● The landscape of the Jezreel Valley in the south of Galilee is characterized by intensive cultivation, which, seen from above, creates rigorous geometric shapes.

464-465 ● In this valley, the countryside seems covered by a patchwork of small and large plots with unique shapes and colors.

466 ● A rainbow of natural colors, made of earth, buds, stems and stalks
in different shades, enlivens the Galilee countryside.

467 ● Waves of sod removed from Issachar Heights are reminiscent of the geometric
patterns of some contemporary art.

An army of bales of hay, deployed out of sight on the surface of a large field, waiting to be harvested.

In an Israeli kibbutz, thousands of red poppies color a field ready for harvest.

472 ● Wheat fields and olive trees are two of the largest components of the Jordan Valley's agricultural wealth.

473 ● The bright yellow of a meadow full of flowers contrasts with the aridity of the hills in the background, which are completely devoid of vegetation.

474 ● Near Be'er Sheva in the Negev, intensive cultivation of fruit trees draws an orderly checkerboard on the land.

475 ● A row of tall cypress trees traces the border between two neighboring fields, protecting the path that runs alongside them with its shadow.

476-477 • Like the blocks of a city, these fields placed close to each other are separated by roads and intersections.

478-479 • In the Jordan Valley, a canal runs through the irrigated fields, bringing precious water for farming activities.

480-481 • The cultivation of olives has for thousands of years represented an important source of livelihood for the inhabitants of the Holy Land.

482-483 • Dry stone walls mark the boundary of fields in which olive trees of different ages grow.

● The circular shape of this huge field, in Kohav in the Jordan Valley, depends on the ingenuity of the irrigation system.

From the surrounding hills, you can enjoy the view of Lake Tiberias and the fertile countryside.

488 ● The absence of vegetation enhances the elegant movement of the geological strata, which are composed of barren hills.

489 ● This mound, which seems like a dome with its perfectly circular perimeter, emerges in a stretch of countryside between the hills of Samaria.

490-491 ● Nature has created its own imaginative mosaic with pieces of green, shades of brown, and earth-colored brushstrokes of ocher.

492-493 ● A small urban settlement seems to disappear, as if it were camouflaged among the rocks on the hills of Samaria.

494-495 ● Poppies and spring flowers celebrate the arrival of the first heat in an olive grove near the Roman city of Umm Qais in Jordan.

INDEX

INDEX

PHOTO CREDITS

PHOTO CREDITS

PHOTO CREDITS

Carlo Giorgi is a journalist and the editor of "Terrasanta" the Italian magazine of the Custody of the Holy Land. To document the day-to-day lives of local Christians, he has made several trips to the Middle East, producing, in that time, a book on Pope Benedict XVI's recent visit to Israel, the Palestinian Territories and Jordan (*Messaggero di Riconciliazione*, Ets 2009). An expert in immigration and social issues, he was director of "Terre di mezzo" and helped produce the Italian-language travel guide *Vado in Senegal!* He has also collaborated with numerous newspapers and magazines in Italy, including "Il Sole 24 Ore".

Cover ● From left:
first rank - Holy Sepulchre, Jerusalem; Wailing Wall and Mosque of Omar, Jerusalem;
Abuhav Synagogue, Safed.
second rank - Lake Tiberias; Masada fortress; view of Jerusalem.
third rank - site of Beit She'an; crusader city of Caesarea Maritima; Herodion hill.

● "Job's Well", between Gehenna and the Kidron Valley, illustrated by David Roberts.

Back cover ● From left:
first rank - Roman aqueduct in Caesarea; view of Acre; monastery of Mar Saba.
second rank - The Damascus Gate, Jerusalem, by David Roberts;
ruins of Herodion; mosaic in Sepphoris, Galilee.
third rank - Mount Tabor; Dead Sea; Holy Sepulchre, Jerusalem.